ALLIANCES AND THE THIRD WORLD

Studies in International Affairs Number 5

Studies in International Affairs Number 5

ALLIANCES AND THE THIRD WORLD

by George Liska

The Washington Center of Foreign Policy Research
School of Advanced International Studies
The Johns Hopkins University

The Johns Hopkins Press, Baltimore

FOREWORD

This essay represents an important facet of the Center's continuing concern to assess basic issues of international politics in the light of new developments. Professor Liska's analysis of the role of alliances in the politics of the less developed countries examines a cross-section of the newest and perhaps most rapidly changing part of the international environment: the relations of the recently independent, economically underdeveloped countries with the major industrial states and with each other. It is a sequel and extended postscript to his own writings on alliances and a companion to three other Center publications: *Alliance Policy in the Cold War* (1959), edited by Arnold Wolfers; *Neutralism and Nonalignment* (1962), edited by Laurence W. Martin; and my forthcoming *Alliances and American Foreign Policy*.

August, 1967   ROBERT E. OSGOOD
                      Director
                      Washington Center of Foreign
                      Policy Research

AUTHOR'S PREFACE

The following essay deals with alliances involving great industrial powers and less developed states. Facing outward toward the global balance of power and inward toward relationships of unequal power among allies, the alliance institution encompasses the problems of contemporary international politics, despite its apparent eclipse as a device of statecraft in the 1960's as compared with the late 1940's and 1950's.

Momentary fashions and speculative long-term trends may be unfavorable to alliances, but the essay expresses a positive and constructive view of them, without ignoring contemporary limitations on their use. The analysis builds upon the author's more extensive discussion of alliances in *Nations in Alliance,* while concentrating on more recent developments and on the less developed segment of the international system.

The discussion begins by describing the international environment and then moves on to consider the functions, determinants, and dynamics of alliances. The middle section deals with alliances joining lesser and greater powers, and the final section discusses alliances of small states only. A short conclusion restates the author's underlying argument by means of a comparison between the ordering role of constitutions within states and that of alliances among them.

CONTENTS

103142

ALLIANCES AND THE THIRD WORLD

Studies in International Affairs Number 5

THE SEGMENTED INTERNATIONAL SYSTEM: THE LESS DEVELOPED COUNTRIES IN WORLD AFFAIRS

I.

Any analysis of the future of alliances in less developed areas will be hampered by two ambiguities and one unknown. The ambiguities concern the very notion of "alliance" as applied to less developed countries in existing and likely conditions, and the general posture of the less developed countries in world politics. The unknown is the state of the international system in a future sufficiently close to make it relevant for present-day planning and sufficiently remote to allow for the crystallization and implementation of new approaches and policies.

The various traditional and modern functions of and motives for alliance will be discussed at a later stage. Suffice it to say initially that the discussion will adhere to an extensive conception of "alliance," going beyond the hard core of an explicit, contractual pledge of military assistance. Apart from traditional looseness in the use of the term "alliance" generally, there are two particular reasons for this license in regard to the less developed countries. The first is that any kind of special tie to a more developed or greater power represents a serious and even risky commitment, comparable in gravity to a contractual undertaking in a more tolerant environment, where alliances are commonplace and considerable secrecy in commitments is feasible. The second reason for using "alliance" loosely—for discussing any kind of alignment and special relationship under the heading of alliances—lies in the disparity of power, ultimately expressed in the quantity and quality of military capability, between the great industrial powers and the less developed countries. Such disparity reduces the importance of reciprocity in pledges of active assistance. It also increases the importance of any conditions that enhance the prospect of using superior military capability with effect, once such use is decided upon.

The posture of the less developed countries in world affairs is both aided and distorted by their coexistence with more advanced and greater industrial powers. The industrial powers of both the West and East supply the less developed countries with models for positive political and organizational action, as well as with some aid toward implementing such action. They also supply the targets for diversionary negative action in the form of psychological aggression. But the industrial powers also distort the relations among the less developed countries. They do so by seeking to impose their own conflicts upon the smaller states and, worse still, by attempting to block the manifestation of the conflicts peculiar to the less developed countries whenever these do not fit into the larger conflict. With regard to alliances, this creates a paradoxical situation. On the one hand the less developed countries can "shop" freely and with relative impunity for forms of alliance policies and for the greater-power allies plentifully supplied by the developed segment of the international system. On the other hand they are undersupplied in regard to the substance of international politics, including that of locally meaningful alliance commitments. Already handicapped by inadequate resources, they are further limited by the extraneous restraints and virtual vetoes of major violence that are more or less imperatively forthcoming from the developed segment, as in the conflict between India and Pakistan and Indonesia's confrontation with Malaysia.

Partly as a result, the more ambitious less developed countries have tended to order their foreign politics around two extremes in order to project power abroad. One extreme consists of the underhanded use of force and craft, such as the subversion and assassination of rival leaders as part of a coup; the dangers of this extreme may grow if isolated nuclear or bacteriological terror weapons become available. Plausible examples are Ghana's policies under Nkrumah and the U.A.R.'s activities in Yemen. The other extreme is the resort to quasi-parliamentary global and regional organizations. These are expected to serve as bases for influence and as expressions of political maturity or of a new and superior type of foreign policy. This gravitation toward extremes is the result of weakness in conventional force and diplomacy. It is in marked and potentially disturbing contrast to the tendency of the greater industrial powers, debarred or discouraged from resorting to extreme expedients, to retreat more frequently to the conventional center of the war-diplomacy spectrum.

The limitations and distortions of the less developed countries' role are all the more significant because these countries are in the formative phase of both their polity and their policy, external as well as internal. Judging by precedents taken from the history of presently advanced states and by current symptoms in some of the less developed countries, the formative phase in the foreign policy of new states would normally entail a strong tendency toward relatively haphazard expansion. Such a phase is characterized by disparity between expansive goals and more limited military means, which have a tendency to shrink when employed. This disparity reduces the need for extraneous checking and balancing by alliances inasmuch as such early forays have limited staying power and are prone to dissolve. Examples are Nasser's U.A.R., Sukarno's Indonesia, Nkrumah's Ghana, and Al Fassi's Morocco (with regard to Mauritania and the Sahara). Even where a major expansionist drive is absent or has failed, the new state will seek in its formative phase to consolidate its territory within "natural" frontiers. It will typically do so by means of policies involving the threat or use of force locally and a tendency to stay aloof from remoter issues and conflicts, which are exploited for national purposes. Examples are Algeria's and Tunisia's early concern over the Sahara, Morocco's over the Spanish enclaves, Pakistan's over Kashmir, and that of other less developed countries, such as Somalia and Thailand, with territorial claims.

Present-day less developed countries are not, as noted, the first to go through such a formative phase. They share with, say, Plantagenet England or Capetian France the undeveloped nature of an internal organization for mobilizing and employing resources in a way commensurate with their expansive or consolidative aims; they share with the early United States the disposition to remain aloof from conflicts in the more developed segment of the international system and, whenever possible, to profit by such conflicts. But they do not have the European powers' advantage of operating in a permissive system which they themselves have defined in conformity with their resources and values. They lack as well the

Americans' advantage of operating on the margin of an "old world" constituting a self-contained multipolar system of mature states, which are able to find stakes of conflict elsewhere while willingly or unwillingly, directly or indirectly, promoting the rising new power's capacity for reshaping the system in due course. In less favorable conditions, a typical less developed country finds it harder progressively to acquire a firm basis in territory and tradition, experience and skills, upon which to build a coherent alliance policy. To be coherent, such a policy would have to go beyond hit-or-miss personal unions between individual leaders, which have an even briefer effect than did comparable marriage alliances of early territorial rulers in Europe.

Beneath the facade of international influence arising from the competition between the major powers, the less developed countries have had difficulties in foreign policy as serious as those encountered in internal economic and political development. Accretion of foreign-policy traditions and skills is an integral part of political development; it would, therefore, be a mistake to treat alignment policies of the less developed countries in relation to the greater powers and among themselves as a redundant distraction from more real and pressing problems. Pending development, many a less developed country will continue to constitute an internally self-contradictory and internationally disturbing compound of elements reminiscent of different stages in the development of the modern state: they will thus display the power drives and methods typical of the Renaissance state; they will be hamstrung by material and social inhibitions characteristic of the feudal polity; they will be forced to contend with the problems of administration and organization (including that of a standing military force) that faced the absolutist dynastic state; and they will be distracted by aspirations associated with the modern reformist welfare state.

Directing attention to the less developed countries merely highlights certain changes in the international system. The basic change since the end of World War II seems to have been a decline in the importance of the ideological factor, a trend that has only been confirmed by Communist China's strident efforts to reassert the role of ideology. Another change has been the reduction of the progressively assimilated nuclear weaponry to a background factor that has no direct impact on most political or even military transactions. This trend seems to be confirmed by the movement from anxiety over nuclear forces already in existence to concern about hypothetical capabilities resulting from further proliferation. The compensatory trend is the increase in the visible significance of industrial power and comparative rates of industrial growth. This is true of the relationship between the industrialized powers and the less developed countries; but it is also true, and with more immediate impact, of the relations between the two unevenly industrialized superpowers themselves. The trend is significant in its own right, aside from the close link between industrial power and both nuclear power and political ideology.

The international system is presently in a fluid state, uncertainly pointing in different directions at once. It continues to be bipolar in the structure of major military and, especially, nuclear power. The bipolarity has, however, been strained in structural as well as policy aspects. Structurally, bipolarity has shrunk and become lopsided. It has been weakened by the diminution of the geopolitical space in which security strategies of third countries are directly and unequivocally related to the military power and balance of the two superpowers. And, even more importantly, despite appearances to the contrary several years earlier, bipolarity has been undermined by the apparent inability of the Soviet Union to move toward economic and technological parity with the United States. Consequently, the system has been acquiring unipolar or, more appropriately, unifocal features. "Bipolarity" has been qualified insofar as the first part of the word implies equality as well as duality and the second part connotes magnetic attraction as well as core of power. In terms of policy, bipolarity has lost some of its underpinning of stakes and, up to a point, rules. It has suffered from the tendency for superpower contests in intermediate areas to cease being meaningful, that is, likely to produce decisive or at least lasting gains for either major contestant. Moreover, in what might appear to be a partial contradiction, it has been proving difficult to abide by one of the key rules of a nonwar bipolar system—to resolve local crises without manifestly humiliating either superpower. So far, the Soviet Union has suffered major prestige setbacks in Cuba, the Congo, and Vietnam. While many a lesser state has been trying to increase local leeway rather than global leverage, the superpowers have tended to lose some of their interest in the less developed countries as their influence declined. Instead, the superpowers have moved to gain leverage over each other by courting major industrial or industrializing allies of the other side—principally France and Communist China—by increased attention, sympathetic or only provisionally hostile. This could not help but give rise to incipient and still uncertain indications of a trend toward multipower diplomacy in a system which has several poles of practically usable power, however much this kind of multipolarity might coexist with, and be recurrently overshadowed by, residual aspects of bipolarity and the emergent features of a unifocal, imperial system centered on the United States.

Moreover, the qualifiedly bipolar system has become even more markedly bisegmental, divided into two classes of political and economic structures and, derivatively, military capabilities. The problem of long-term coexistence between industrially and politically developed and undeveloped segments has moved to the foreground. This shift in the character of the principal systemic crisis has coincided with, and was largely due to, the routinization of the cold war between the two superpowers and to the more general tendency of all the industrialized powers to progress toward a relatively civilized mode of reciprocal relations. The problem is not unprecedented. A developed Italian state system in the fifteenth and sixteenth centuries coexisted with a less developed northern monarchial segment in Europe. In the contemporary instance, however, political underdevelopment and relative weakness happen to coincide as they did not in the earlier case. Moreover, except intermittently in critical areas such as the Middle East and Southern Asia, alliances across the lines of segmentation are even less likely to promote the interpenetration and integration of the two segments in ways that would be meaningful, even if unevenly advantageous, for countries in both segments.

The coexistence between, and political integration of, the developed and the undeveloped segments have been hampered by some factors and facilitated by others. A negative factor has been the so-called widening gap in economic growth. In this respect foreign material assistance may not have compensated entirely for the traditional security incentives to development and military modes of selection between viable and nonviable entities; both development and selection have been hampered by limitations on the use of force emanating from the more advanced powers. Conversely, the narrowing gap between alignment and nonalignment, to be discussed later, may prove to have a positive influence. The political counterpart of uneven economic development, with likewise adverse effects, has been the successive emergence of the United States, Japan, the U.S.S.R., and China as "new" world powers, and their performance today at different levels of saturation and with varying awareness of wider responsibility. This situation is characteristic of emerging international systems, of which the contemporary world system is an example. A corresponding adverse feature is the continuing dearth of nearly equal, mature, and internationally conservative states, which tend to control an international system in mid-career, between emergence and decline. The positive feature in this respect is the currently low incidence of the key difficulty besetting an overripe international system: the prevalence of declining powers tending to take the international system with them in their fitful attempts to avert decay. The more stagnant of the undeveloped countries might eventually display some of the impulses of the declining states, but it is unlikely that these states would have the capacity to impress their plight upon the system in its entirety.

As so far presented, the basic global structures of power and the national policy orientations are compatible with a variety of alternative international environments. Such environments can be differentiated by three features—the distribution of power, key conflicts, and principles of order—which condition the role of alliances.

The more important range concerns the developed, or rapidly developing, greater powers. In terms of the above criteria, the range encompasses at least three possible environments. One would consist of continued, though uneven or fluctuating, bipolarity (with some departures toward tripolarity); dominance of the East-West conflict (with the Soviet Union or Communist China as the principal, or momentarily determining, adversary of the United States); and stalemate as the basis of elementary order. The second possible environment would consist of a tendency toward multipolarity in the distribution of power as well as of policy initiatives and influence; flexible and limited competition among the greater powers (including competition between the United States and its nominal or former allies) over the allocation of influence and conditions of order in Europe and the undeveloped areas; and elements of great-power concert as the basic principle of order. The third possible environment would display an accentuated tendency toward a unifocal system—that is, over-all global predominance by one world power—representing the principal source of order as well as the target of countervailing efforts by the lesser major powers jointly or individually in particular regions.

The variants are neither exhaustive nor mutually exclusive in all aspects; and they are not necessarily independent of the alternatives for the less developed countries. These alternatives can be defined along the same lines as those concerning the greater powers. Power might be widely dispersed in the pursuit of regional integration; key conflicts among or including less developed countries would then be decreasingly military; and the basic principle of order would be functional and institutional cooperation toward collective power and welfare (in cooperation with ex-metropoles or other assistance-supplying states). Alternatively, there might be a reversion to traditional patterns of territorial and other conflicts among relatively equal and weak powers, as part of the crystallization of regional subsystems (rather than organizations). An evolving intraregional hierarchy and balance of power would extend into the central global system and constitute the key principles of order. Yet another possibility is accelerated movement toward differentiation of power and intensification of conflict along racial lines. This might occur as part of the conflict strategy of major nonwhite powers, or it might represent a spontaneous reaction of less developed countries to sharp decreases in development aid, while the industrialized nonwhite powers are assimilated into a great-power concert that reduces competitive incentives to such aid. Any existing degree of order in this last case would be based on the insufficiency of resources underlying more or less opportunistic actions on behalf of racial equality.

The relationship between existing American alliance policies and the different global environments is perforce hypothetical. It would seem, for instance, that existing alliance policies would be most nearly preserved in the first variants, that is, in stalemated

East-West bipolarity for the industrial powers and regional integration politics oriented toward economic development for the nonindustrial powers. Substantial recasting of alignments and reinterpretation of commitments to play down the ideological factor would probably attend the second variants. These encompass a mildly competitive, concert-oriented multipolar system in the industrial segment, and regional subsystems characterized by conventional territorial conflicts and balance of power politics in the undeveloped segment. The anti-Communist alliances of the United States with Iran, Pakistan, or Thailand, for instance, would hardly flourish in such an environment. The combination of the third variants—a unifocal or imperial global system with a tendency toward racially defined conflicts and politics in the undeveloped segment—might well call for even greater changes in existing alignments, so as to implement the principle of impartiality as well as keep a free hand for the imperial power faced with a multitude of volatile local conflicts and disorders. Only in the industrial segment might the tendency toward one-power predominance be compatible with a mere change in the spirit of existing alliances. The change in the West might be toward greater subordination to the United States or, alternately, toward greater leeway for lesser allies to combine ultimate military commitment and dependence with considerable freedom for countervailing politico-economic action (on the supposition that the United States would be the globally predominant power in the near future).

The relationship between existing alliances and alternative environments becomes even more uncertain when we introduce varying states of nuclear diffusion. These range from widespread and indiscriminate dissemination, through nuclear oligopoly of major industrialized states, to continued duopoly of the superpowers marginally modified by inferior nuclear capabilities of a few middle powers. East-West bipolar conflict might then coexist with conventional territorial conflicts in the undeveloped, "southern" segment, in conditions of nuclear duopoly; or a competitive concert among the great powers might coexist with a tendency toward ideological and racial conflict in the undeveloped segment, in conditions of indiscriminate diffusion of nuclear capabilities on different levels of sophistication.

Rather than examine all the possible variations,[1] the author will instead describe the "mixed" international environment, which is most likely to eventuate in a future for which it is at all possible to plan and prepare.

The most likely international environment of the future is one in which the United States exercises over-all global primacy grounded in more exclusive paramountcy in the Western Hemisphere. Other powers would exercise or aspire to primacy or paramountcy within other individual regions or subregional areas. Such an international system would differ from two plausible alternative systems: one in which the two superpowers dominate within their respective blocs while contending on equal terms over unassigned areas; another in which the United

---

[1] I have treated some aspects of nuclear proliferation in Alden Williams, ed., *Arms, Science and Politics* (Columbus, Ohio: forthcoming). The following description of a "mixed" international environment is conformable with, but may be complemented by, the more extensive discussion of the international system and order in the author's *Imperial America* (Baltimore, Md.: 1967), pp. 10ff., 36ff.

States would seek to go beyond global primacy to outright dominance based on paramountcy in all or most of the world's regions. The distinction is elusive but essential. "Primacy" connotes status as first or foremost, but not necessarily hegemonial or paramount, power. The existence of such power was the common experience of the European state system as it moved beyond its primitive origins. The foremost power (France, Spain, France again, Germany) was, in principle, capable of defeating all the other states militarily, but was hemmed in most of the time by the existence of foreign interests and conflicts that could not be administered by constant recourse to force on a vast scale. When major wars did occur, the foremost power was typically prevented from converting primacy into domination by the action of a normally dormant or otherwise occupied reserve power from outside the system's core—England, the United States, and, before she herself became "European" and a candidate for primacy, Russia.

In the anticipated international system, the twin capacity underlying primacy—to assert military power with considerable effect as a last resort while influencing political conditions constantly—would continue to be circumscribed on both the global and regional planes. The global primacy of the United States would be limited by the special position of local powers in the different regions other than the Western Hemisphere. This would tend to reduce American political influence while raising the level of military conflict in which the globally foremost (but not regionally paramount) power would be inclined to intervene or be capable of intervening with decisive effect. The regional primacy of other powers would in turn be limited by the risk that an excessive exercise of political influence would make local resistance assume a forcible expression, and by the related risk that every increase in the level of military violence would increase the prospect of American intervention and decrease the prospects of a conclusion favorable to the foremost regional power or powers. In consequence, the politics of such a multipower and multiregional system, resting on what might be called the equilibrium of complementary (global and regional) imbalances under the leadership of a primary world power, would thus be the function of two related factors. One is the ability, notably of the United States, to retain or secure access to individual regional theaters by means and under conditions short of total war, especially while the precise shape of the new world order is being defined; the other is the effective recourse to extraregional power by lesser states in the different regions.[2]

The proliferation of nuclear weapons would not basically change the pattern, although it would introduce new problems of deterrence and control. Nuclear weapons may remain confined to the greater industrial powers. The likely result would be stalemate based on multilateral deterrence among regional nuclear powers and nuclear imbalance between the United States and any single regional nuclear power. In either case, the United States as a global power and even some lesser extraregional powers are likely to retain access to the region for purposes of influence or intervention. If nuclear weapons spread to

[2] See the author's *Europe Ascendant* (Baltimore, Md.: 1964), p. 167, referring to "the development of a new multipolar order in which the leading powers would work out the modalities of reciprocal access to areas adjoining the several heartlands."

nonindustrial states, they are not likely to be sufficiently significant to affect the regional and global balances of power and deterrence among the industrial states. Should instability and abuse result, however, the great nuclear powers would be under pressure to proceed to some form of control action in ways that reinforce existing trends toward a great-power concert.[3]

As of now, the world system is divided into regions of different kinds. In one class of regions the issue of primacy is settled and likely to remain so for some time. The Western Hemisphere and Eastern Europe are such regions, although in both of them the political or policy issue of access by and recourse to powers from outside the region is only beginning to evolve. In another class of regions the issue of primacy is not settled in terms of either power structure or policy. In Western Europe, primacy may finally remain vested in the United States, fall to a local power, or, in an all-Europe framework, go to Soviet Russia. In South Asia the most likely powers to contest for primacy are China, Japan, India, and, secondarily, Soviet Russia as an Asian power and eventually perhaps Australia (with American backing). Their contest will facilitate the effort of the United States—which as a global power is also a Pacific power—to retain not only access to the region but also the capacity to participate in the contest over regional primacy. In Africa no manifestly greater regional powers have emerged so far. The U.A.R. and Algeria may well be increasingly handicapped by racial differences from Black Africa; Ni-

---

[3] See the author's discussion of "adversary" and "cooperative" superpower control in Williams' *Arms, Science and Politics*.

geria has been beset by internal divisions and South Africa by racial problems. It is possible that Africa will divide into at least three subregions: Arab North (Maghreb and the Near East), contended over by Algeria and Egypt; one or several Black African subregions in the middle zone; and a white-dominated south with South Africa as its core. In such a case, extraregional powers would face the problem of access to primacy conflicts within such regions and subregions as well as to racial conflicts among them.

As part of the change in both bipolarity and the East-West conflict, the gap between alliance and nonalignment is likely to narrow. As a policy, nonalignment consisted of refusal to enter into formal and permanent alliance or alignment with either party to the East-West conflict. Its militant, neutralist expression was marked by a systematic effort to exploit the conflict between the two superpowers. It entailed a preference for keeping a free hand also in regard to local and regional issues not directly related to the cold war.

Globally, nonalignment and neutralism thrived on several factors. First of all, the superpowers saw their conflict as one over multiregional primacy, that is, as if primacy or paramountcy in all regions were to fall ultimately to one superpower. Success consequently meant converting nonaligned powers to alignment or, at least, making them tolerate the alliances that a superpower acquired as a basis for paramount position in a particular region. Second, thriving nonalignment depended on a definite superpower military technology—one which put a premium on established, permanent local facilities and on nonmilitary, politico-economic modes of contest over local states. The third and final precondition was the political inexperience of the United States and the Soviet Union as the "new," noncolonial great powers in dealings with "new" lesser states, whose leaders were quite well versed in the old methods of balancing and blackmailing statecraft. All these underpinnings have been crumbling. Neutralism may well go down in history as a shrewd but rather crude policy of newly independent countries presuming to base a foreign-policy doctrine on transient conditions which include the relatively primitive military technology of politically unsophisticated major powers.

In addition to changes in the global conditions of nonalignment there have been changes in regional conditions. In regions where a local greater power has bid for primacy, though not yet conclusively (thus is South Asia claimed by Communist China), the superpower confrontation has receded into the background. Nonalignment, losing its foundations, has been veering toward alignment as the danger increased that a free hand might come to mean an empty and unarmed hand. For different forms of self-protection and assistance, various nonaligned states have moved toward alignment—Burma and Cambodia with China, Indonesia first with China and subsequently with small-state neighbors, and India with the United States and the Soviet Union. But also in regions where no local power has yet meaningfully bid for primacy, as in Africa, the limitations of nonalignment have been progressively revealed, not least on the part of former spearheads of neutralism. The reasons have been many: growing internal weakness in economic subsistence, as in the U.A.R., and in political stability, as in Ghana and Guinea; external military involvement, as by the U.A.R. in Yemen as part of a bid for subregional primacy; and internal military coups in both French- and English-speaking Africa. Consequently, there has been greater self-restraint in relations with less long-suffering superpowers, as a matter of necessity on the part of chastened neutralists or as a matter of policy on the part of new military incumbents. And there has been a greater or more frankly admitted ultimate dependence on ex-metropoles for economic and military assistance.

The situation has been different in regions where the primacy issue was apparently settled. Here the trend has been away from rigid alignment and integration toward less alignment with the leading superpower, leaving open the possibility for a politically freer hand in conditions short of an acute military threat. Present examples are Rumania in Eastern Europe, France in Western Europe, and, say, Canada at one extreme and Cuba at the other in the Western Hemisphere.

The unifying trend has been toward less conspicuous forms of military cooperation. This has meant, between allies, an evolution toward less rather than more military integration in peacetime; with technically nonaligned countries, it has meant an evolution toward improvised, highly mobile military assistance to meet urgent security needs, such as the airlifts to India. A parallel trend has been toward often conspicuous political and economic cooperation or coordination between allies and nonallies. Intensified nonmilitary cooperation has been propagated as a supplement to undeveloped or fading military links between allies, as in SEATO and NATO, respectively. But it has been most marked between nonallies such as France and the Soviet Union, the United States and India. Such *rapproche-*

ments have served as an alternative to military links and as tentative first steps toward possible future alignments with presently unavowed or unavowable security implications. In these circumstances, the gap between alignment and nonalignment is much attenuated; so is, as a consequence, the particular dilemma for policy, notably of the United States, which in the heyday of neutralism could plausibly be formulated in terms of antithetical strategies of conciliation and discrimination vis-à-vis neutralists.[4]

---

[4] See the author's *Nations in Alliance* (Baltimore, Md.: 1962), pp. 237ff.

103142

I. THE BALANCE OF POWER AND PREPONDERANT POWER: ALLIANCES OF SMALL AND GREAT POWERS

Alliances are the institutional link between the politics of the balance of power and the politics of preponderance or empire. The corresponding formal distinction may, but need not always, be one between equal and unequal alliances. The material difference concerns the principal or distinctive purpose of an alliance. As an institutional device an alliance may aim chiefly at augmenting one's insufficient power or it may be intended to control the ally's use of power even while supplementing it. The following chapters, without ignoring the balance-of-power aspect of alliances, will stress the role of alliances in the spectrum of instrumentalities available to a preponderant power such as the United States. In the process, we shall concentrate on the functions, determinants, and dynamics of alliances comprising the less developed countries. After discussing alliances that place these countries in the company of more developed and bigger powers, we shall turn to alliances that do not include big powers.

What are likely to be the functions of alliances and alignments and consequently their determinants (including the motives of policy-makers) within the anticipated international environment? The question could be dismissed with the answer: none, on two main grounds. First, alliances are unnecessary if military cooperation can be improvised in the case of actual attack on a nonaligned state, because of the increasing mobility and firepower of conventional weapons; second, alliances will soon prove unacceptable to nuclear powers individually and infeasible among them collectively if proliferation takes its course, except provisionally in the form of nuclear guarantees designed to slow down or regulate the spread of nuclear weapons. The simple, negative answer will not necessarily prove to be wrong in the end; at this point, however, there is still need for a somewhat more elaborate analysis.

The functions of alliance were varied even in the heyday of conventionally armed diplomacy. Implicit in these functions always is the threat against which the alliance guards. We must identify the traditional functions before we judge their relevance for future relations. The functions can be classified as bearing on aggregation of power, interallied control, and international order or government.

As a vehicle for the aggregation of power, an alliance is first and foremost a means for adding interchangeable, cumulative military power. This is the basic additive function of alliances and needs no illustration. It is implemented by means of pacts of mutual assistance or guarantees intended to safeguard individual powers against superior adversary power and the international system against severe imbalance and hegemony. A special case of power aggregation by alliance occurs when the alliance serves to project influence by way of accessible states toward states having more affinity with the ally than with the principal power. A major purpose may then be to guard against polarizing the system on religious, ideological, racial, or other grounds. France's alliances with Protestant German states or Sweden in the Thirty Years' War were such alliances, as have been her more recent pacts with French-speaking African states.

The second major function is interallied control. It will underlie most characteristically those alliances meant to maximize surveillance over an otherwise undependable power. The purpose is to safeguard the contracting party or parties against betrayal, counteralliance, and the like in conditions of great instability and capacity for surprise action. The practice of diplomatic representation originated in this kind of alliance context in Renaissance Italy.

A more conventional and persistent control is implemented by an alliance intended to exercise restraint over an ally by way of reassurance. One of the allies proposes, then, to safeguard himself against the unstabilizing behavior of a restless or a declining power. Examples are the Dual Alliance of 1879 between Germany and Austria-Hungary and Britain's alliances with France at various points, beginning in 1715. What is an implicit right to restrain in an alliance between equal allies can become an explicit right to intervene in unequal alliances designed to legitimize intervention. The specific purpose may be to safeguard the allied actors against domestic opponents. Such was the case in the Anglo-Iraqi alliance of the 1930's and, much earlier, in Spain's alliance with French Catholics in religious wars. The Spanish case shows that such an alliance may be with nongovernmental actors if the authoritative government is in abeyance.

The third and last major function of alliance is to promote international order or even international government. Here belongs, first, an alliance meant to legitimize or strengthen one or both allied regimes as a safeguard against the spread of domestic instabilities. A related purpose may be to check the need for aggressive external diversions from contests over internal authority. In such a case, the international-order function overlaps with the interallied-control function. Among possible examples are the alliance between the actual or hopeful successor regimes, the Hanoverians in England and the Orleans in France, in the aftermath of the wars of Louis XIV, and, more recently, the Conseil de l'Entente in modern Africa. Promotion of international order comes close to being international government if an alliance institutionalizes a "concert" among great powers and is used to deal with interstate conflict as well as with more fundamental threats such as social revolution. The classic instance is the Quadruple Alliance at the end of the Napoleonic Wars; a more recent one is the stillborn Four-Power Pact of 1934 designed to effect revision of the Versailles peace settlement. In a narrower framework, finally, an alliance may amount to a quasi-constitutional union and serve as a safeguard against desperate recourses or internal collapse of the less viable allied state or regime. This kind of alliance may also serve to transfer primacy from a declining to a rising state. Examples are the projects of Anglo-Dutch union in the mid-seventeenth century, the Austro-German Dual Alliance of 1879, and, in some aspects, the Ghana-Guinea union schemes of the 1960's.

The functions of alliances have been indicated so far without differentiating between greater and lesser powers. Implicit in these functions are the motives of actors to enter into a particular alliance—the subjective side of the determinants of alliance. They will be examined now with regard to alliances be-

tween greater and lesser powers, first from the viewpoint of the lesser states and subsequently from that
of the greater powers.

The motives of lesser powers to ally with great
powers can be summed up under the heading of security, stability, and status.

Security can be threatened either by comparable
lesser powers or by clearly superior powers. In the
first case, a lesser state may or may not be capable of
relating its conflict to conflicts of greater states in
such a way as to aggregate power and maintain or
even aggrandize its national territory (or any other
element determining relative standing). Most less
developed countries have actually been reluctant to
relate their local conflicts to the global East-West
conflict; Pakistan did, but was reluctant to subordi-
nate the local conflict (with India) to the global one.
There have been several reasons for this reluctance.
Only the non-Communist fragments of partitioned
lesser countries have had acute conflicts with Com-
munist-controlled small countries which could be
fought out in the open. The superpowers have increasingly tended to cooperate with the desire of the
smaller powers to keep other conflicts—between Pakistan and India, Morocco and Algeria, Indonesia and
Malaysia, the U.A.R. and Saudi Arabia and, with
qualifications, even that between the Arabs and
Israel—separate from the great-power rivalry.
Moreover, most of the actual or prospective small-
state "aggressors" (Israel being one of the few ex-
ceptions) have been incapable of sustaining effective
military action over any substantial length of time.
This has decreased the need of the "victim" for
great-power alliances in crisis, as compared with the
need for military supplies prior to crises for the pur-

pose of roughly equalizing the adversary's low-level and dissolution-prone capabilities. As for security against greater hegemonic powers, some of the less developed countries have come to face (or feel that they face) more than one such threat, either directly or indirectly via a lesser-power ally of the great powers. Should a country like Pakistan seek protection against the global hegemonic threat of the Soviet Union or the United States, the regional threat from Communist China, or the subregional, local threat from India? No great-power alliance is apt to serve against all these threats, a fact which cannot but depreciate any formal, exclusive great-power alliance from Pakistan's viewpoint. On the other hand, small states with a manifest security threat (Thailand, for example) continue to show great interest in alliance with a great power or in the guarantees of a great power, as in the case of Cuba and the states in the Arabian peninsula.

The second major motive for alliance is concern for stability. Ever since the beginning of anything like a European state system, alliances have been related to the supply of economic assets for the decisive political actor, be it prince or people. Thus, in the early fourteenth century, financial subsidies to princes in the Low Countries and wool supplies for Flemish cities played a major role in the English alliance system that initiated the Hundred Years' War. At least three factors currently undercut the role of supply (meaning, chiefly, economic aid) to less developed countries. The first is the existence of more than one alternative source; another is the tendency of the superpowers to abjure alliance commitment as the ostensible criterion for apportioning aid; and the third is the difficulty of using the supply of foodstuffs as a political instrument—on the pattern of Ottoman grain supplies for Venice—in regard to societies haunted by the problem of famine. Conversely, the prospect of political assistance to allied incumbents, of doubtful value at the peak of neutralist agitation, may now again be assigned a greater value following the decline of both postcolonial stability and the antineocolonialist scare. British interventions for political stability in Kenya and Tanganyika in the 1960's parallel similar obligations and performance in regard to newly independent Iraq in the 1930's. To an increasing number of less developed countries, selectively disengaged ex-metropolitan powers may be more efficient and more tolerable great-power allies in the search for postindependence stability than superpowers without colonial antecedents, as long as the ex-metropoles retain the capacity and will for instant but limited re-engagement. By contrast, too deep an involvement of a great-power ally, such as that of the United States in South Korea and Vietnam, always threatens to reduce the great-power ally's capacity for promoting political stability at critical junctures.

The final motive for a small state's alliance with a great power is an increase in status. It did operate, for instance, in the case of the governments in the Balkans before World War I and in Central-Eastern Europe afterward (to cite relatively recent examples of newly independent states), but it suffered a marked eclipse after World War II. It is not impossible, however, that status considerations may again come to foster alignments in a genuinely postcolonial international system, especially one informally governed by a primary power, a great-power concert, or a combination of the two.

Alliances between unequal powers have been, and will for some time continue to be, conditioned by adverse factors such as cultural differences between actual or potential allies, great disparity in the level and nature of military power, and low dependability of less developed countries in alliances and other forms of state behavior. Most or all of these aspects have tended to prevail as normal during long periods of time. One exception applies to hardware before the nineteenth century. Then, relatively primitive and static military technology enabled many a small state to match much bigger powers in the composition and level of military power. Another exception can be discerned in the short period between the two world wars. Relations between France and her small-state allies were then marked by relative geographic and cultural propinquity, qualitative identity and quantitative comparability of military power, and high dependability of the small-state allies. Insofar and as long as they prevail, the negative factors will and ought to affect the motivation of greater powers to ally with lesser powers. The key motives of great powers to enter into "unequal alliances" can be summed up in terms of aggregation or addition, diversion, and disguise of power and its exercise.

The basic motive, that of the additional power of lesser allies, is no longer necessarily the primary one. It has actually been on the decline ever since the commitment of Swiss contingents ceased to determine the balance of power among the territorially larger powers in the mid-sixteenth century. Small states did, of course, continue to represent a significant potential addition of power until the end of the eighteenth century. At the outset of the twentieth century, they again provided valuable active contingents and, most recently, vital facilities for greater allies. The present situation is ambiguous. On the one hand, existing and probable future military technology tends to depreciate radically the additive capacity of smaller states, even in regard to bases and related facilities. On the other hand, the growing importance of the cultural and racial factor attending the rise of regional powers like China cannot but enhance the utility of alliances with remote lesser states. They are a source of locally suitable manpower and legitimation, even though contingents may be small and be further dwarfed as a conflict escalates. Thai cooperation and the South Korean contingent in Vietnam have illustrated this point.

Even where aggregation as an incentive is insignificant, the desire to divert small-state power from alliance with an adversary may suffice to motivate what would then be a preclusive alliance. This consideration entered heavily into Britain's traditional interest in Portugal as an ally, for instance. To divert a smaller state from an alternative alignment may be especially important for powers outside a region in a contest over primacy in regional orbits, the reason being that the capacity of a great power indigenous to the region to engage less developed local countries in alliance may well create the undesired impression of irresistible advance toward regional primacy. In such a case it would matter little that the power increment represented by the less developed countries was small or that the small allies might even constitute an outright economic and political liability for the local greater power. It suffices here to recall the initial impression created by China's advance toward alignments with Indonesia, Pakistan, and Cambodia up to 1966. On the other hand, even a burdensome alliance of an extraregional great power with a small state will be a worthwhile objective and gain if the small state was previously within the orbit of an adversary great power. Examples are Yugoslavia's semialignment with the United States and Cuba's twin alignment with the Soviet Union and Communist China. In the short run, such alliances can help divert the resources and attention of the bested great power from the winner's small-state allies nearer home; in the long run, they may represent a key asset in a global contest over the final structure of a regionalized world order. Only at a later stage in the evolution of such a world order, when the relationships of control and access by greater powers and recourse to them by the smaller ones have been stabilized, might a lesser state be able to assert independence from a regionally dominant great power without being pulled into compensatory alignment with another, presumably remoter, great power. The experience of Rumania may prove interesting in this respect.

The final major motive for a great power to enter into alliance with a smaller power—next to adding and diverting power—is to disguise its control over the lesser ally's actions. The actual purposes of such an alliance may be as varied as hegemonial dominance, restraint to foster equilibrium and peace, and surveillance to guard against disastrous ventures or surprises. Among these alliances were Russia's with Serbia before World War I as well as those of the United States in Latin America, France in French-speaking Africa, and the Soviet Union in Eastern Europe. This class of motives is relatively independent from the state of conflicts among great powers. It may, therefore, gain in relative importance as the other motivations weaken with diminution of major conflicts. It may come to loom very large in the future should conflicts among small states intensify and nuclear weapons spread or threaten to spread to the less developed countries.

Even such a pressing motive for alliance with a less developed country as disguise of control need not, of course, insure small-power cooperation any more reliably than did the more traditional concerns. In this connection, the question may be raised as to whether control over nuclear weaponry in the context of nuclear proliferation would constitute an original and unprecedented basic motive for alliance or would be one of several such motives. From the viewpoint of lesser countries, ideological affinity, say between Cuba and the U.S.S.R., may constitute a vital supplement to traditional motives (to wit, supply of material aid for stability and military backing for security, increase in status as a result of an alliance contracted in defiance of the hegemonic power). Historically fostered cultural affinities between ex-metropoles and former colonies might likewise rate as newly significant. Such incentives, however, are not substantially different from confessional incentives to particular alignments during the religious wars, and they are not sufficient grounds for alliance, although they may help to consolidate alliances entered into and held together by more concrete and pragmatic considerations. The nuclear factor, by contrast, may constitute something of a novelty, especially if a special guarantee against the use of nuclear military power by a local adversary comes to be held technically compatible with "nonalignment" in the conventional dimensions of politics and military technology.

The nuclear factor may motivate greater powers to ally with lesser ones in order to inhibit nuclear dispersion as well as exert surveillance in peacetime and control in wartime over an already nuclearized lesser state. In a larger sense, great powers may welcome alliances primarily as a basis from which to be admitted to, and exercise leverage in, the management of conflicts among lesser powers in a difficult-to-master military-technological, ideological, and cultural context. Such a concern may become more significant in contemporary practice than the desire to use alliance as a means for conversion to an ideology or reconversion to colonial status. America's alliance with Pakistan, for instance, may be increasingly justified in these terms; conversely, the alliance has served the Pakistani government as a basis for attenuating the domestic implications of failure to finally "settle" the Kashmir conflict politically or militarily by facilitating relatively risk-free diversionary maneuvers, such as exploring alternatives to, as well as shifting blame onto, a noncooperative or even inhibiting (but still vital) great-power ally. A comparable case might be made for the Soviet alignment with the U.A.R. and the American one with Israel.

It would thus seem that significant grounds do remain for alliances between industrialized great powers and the less developed small states, especially if functions and motives are broadly interpreted. The relative importance of grounds having to do with military insecurity and those bearing on politico-economic stability will depend on the precise character of international environment. But certainly it will not prove to be more correct or politically feasible to equate security with development than it would be to ignore development for military security.[1] Alliances and alignments serving primarily the purposes of politico-economic development may prove to be even more unstable than alliances rooted in military considerations, insofar as development entails a variation in internal regimes and external orientations. Even those alliances oriented toward development will be stable only if the greater-power ally remains manifestly able (even if less manifestly willing) to convert politico-economic backing into military support in a great crisis.

The prospects for alliances among greater and lesser powers are not all favorable, however. They are qualified by unfavorable developments of the past. They are, therefore, contingent upon a positive estimate of the policy-makers' ability to adjust to past failings and future requirements.

The often unfavorable dynamics of alliances among unequal powers have had to do chiefly with the consolidation of alliances and their repercussions in domestic politics. The major multilateral alliance comprising less developed countries, SEATO, was never consolidated. Unlike NATO, it failed even to develop an initial momentum that could be tested by subsequent crises. By contrast, consolidation of formally or *de facto* bilateral American alliances with South Korea, the Philippines, and Thailand (the latter as the only surviving component of SEATO), has come to mean American overinvolvement. This has militated against eventual transfer of some responsibilities to a friendly regional power, such as Japan in regard to South Korea. In the case of SEATO, initiation was followed almost immediately by symp-

[1] See "Address of Secretary of Defense Robert S. McNamara before the American Society of Newspaper Editors," *The New York Times*, May 19, 1966, p. 11.

toms of accelerated dissolution as the delay in the coming of acute crisis in the area produced a faltering of the original purpose. At the same time, no serious attempt was made to infuse life into the alliance by diverting its thrust to substitute functions, such as economic development, even at the cost of "duplicating" other agencies functionally more specific and politically less handicapped.

SEATO suffered from several interconnected mismanagements aside from the unavoidable disparity of material power among allies and their dependence for cohesion on the level of pressures exerted by the target state. One was the incongruity between an excessive propagandistic and institutional buildup of the alliance, which had been devised as a substitute for forceful action in 1954, and the failure to develop it during the short initial period of favorable convergence of manageable Communist pressure and considerable local interest (on the part of Thailand and the so-called protected states, Laos, Cambodia, and South Vietnam) as a basis for action in 1964. The failure to involve the interested lesser states in a cooperative effort with economic and prestige payoffs, after they had been compromised by their engagement, encouraged extreme vacillation in attitudes toward the alliance on the part of the least engaged countries, the so-called protocol states. This failure was largely responsible for the decline of interest in the alliance on the part of the relatively most-committed member, Thailand, while it projected the issue of loyalty to a not clearly advantageous alliance into the Thai domestic struggle for power; it also strengthened the less immediately concerned Asian allies, the Philippines and Pakistan, in their attitude of noncooperative indifference. Yet another misjudgment was to combine the policy of alliance with less developed countries with that of wooing nonaligned countries conspicuously hostile to the alliance, notably India, and with a posture of deference to the competence of less cold-war-oriented organizations. While the Colombo Plan was favored in regard to economic development, the United Nations was given preference in regard to at least one security issue clearly concerning the alliance: investigation of alleged North Vietnamese infiltration in Laos in 1959, originally requested from the alliance by the Laos government.[2] The subordination was in sharp contrast to the American conception of the balance of responsibilities between the United Nations and another regional alliance, the Organization of American States, in matters of regional security.

In view of this mismanagement, SEATO—like CENTO and some bilateral American alliances—lent itself easily to condemnation as a functionless alliance that, on the whole, was harmful to exposed lesser states because it incited subversive action rather than deterred overt aggression. Once overt formalized alliances between unequal states fail visibly to foster military security and stability, however, their intangible effects assume inordinate importance. Among such effects will be the disorder introduced into the internal as well as the interstate politics of a country with a primitive polity and economy by an alliance with an industrialized great

[2] See George Modelski, ed., *SEATO* (Canberra: 1962), pp. 11–12, 76, 149–50, and *passim* for a general analysis. SEATO's subsequent "impotency and lack of will" regarding Laos was pointedly recalled by the Thai Foreign Minister in 1966 in the context of South Vietnam. See *The New York Times,* June 28, 1966, p. 3.

state. As the foremost industrial power the United States has sought to compensate both its less developed allies and the nonaligned opponents of its alliances for the perhaps inevitable dislocations. These efforts, however, have not served to reduce the material gap between the unequally developed countries. Instead, they have prematurely narrowed the political gap between states of unequal power by raising the less developed countries to an artificially high level of apparent importance and influence. Such an elevated position is difficult or impossible to sustain in the long run. Moreover, it represents a distraction from internal tasks and manageable local foreign-policy concerns, a fact which only aggravates the original disorder. From the viewpoint of the United States, some of its most conspicuous alliances have failed to insure either disguised control (witness South Korea under Rhee and, even more so, South Vietnam under Diem) or ostentatious deterrence (note the SEATO military exercises over the years). The less effective such alliances are in realizing their purposes, however, the stronger is the case for non-ostentatious alliances with minimum peacetime impact.

Considering past failings and continuing needs, the question may be raised at this point: What are the future prospects of alliances between unequal powers in terms of the three principal grounds for alliance—national power aggregation, interstate control, and international order or government? We can try to answer the question in terms of a mid-point conclusion.

In order to aggregate national power, alliances between great powers and less developed countries must do certain things. On the material side, they must promote the development of the less developed allies in preference to other lesser countries, notably in the grace period before powers indigenous to a region become both disposed and strong enough to inhibit extraregional supply. This may mean "unilateral aid now, mutual assistance later." If military action against a threat becomes mandatory, meaningful aggregation can occur only on a level adjusted to the resources of the less developed countries, without necessarily descending to the so-called subconventional level of fighting. On the political side, satisfactory aggregation of national capabilities presupposes complementarity of the relevant interstate conflicts and national concerns. The alliance should be shaped so as to take into account and, ideally, deal with the conflict concerns of the less developed country or countries. It will be increasingly rare for such local conflicts to reflect the dominant global conflict. Only by diminishing the ideological, anti-Communist basis of American commitments might national concerns of potential or desirable less developed allies and the American stake in international order come to coincide. Specific commitments might then be conveniently framed and implemented so as to come into operation only against manifestly superior power—that is, when a great power or two or more lesser powers are pitted against the country aligned with the United States or protected by it.

The vital issue is how to relate the greater power to local conflicts in such a way as to reconcile power aggregation with great-power control without prejudicing the development needs of the lesser countries. This may call for the reduction of great-power restraints on contests between comparable small states whenever imperative restraint would impede the development of political self-consciousness and the crystallization of regional subsystems. Such reserve would not result in the complete suspension of inter-state control any more than it would call for abandoning opposition to forcible expressions of local imperialisms. The resolution of the undeniable dilemma may be found in one experience. An outside power can often best influence the negotiations for peaceful settlement if it has previously guaranteed the lesser state against total defeat and obliteration even if not against all setbacks or against failure to satisfy maximum goals. Holding the ring for a lesser ally is to render him, and the alliance, better service on occasion than would be the case if he were held back at all costs. In the long run, this may prove to be a vital point for America's relationship with Israel. Likewise, the right to exert surveillance over the use or nonacquisition of nuclear weapons by a small state may well be contingent on a prior commitment to provide substitute means of security, just as preferential economic aid as part of an alliance concerned primarily with stability is the necessary, although, judging by recent experience, not the sufficient, prerequisite for effective advice and guidance. An alliance supplies the undeniable justification and the irremovable sanction for the exercise of control; actual authority has to be supplied by those who implement the alliance at the summit and in the field. Peremptory cease-fire orders, treaties against nuclear dissemination, or allegedly nonpolitical multilateral agencies for development aid reflect the desire of some or all greater powers to exercise international government without local involvement. It is unlikely, however, that in the foreseeable future any such streamlined devices will suffice to perform the control function between the unequal segments of the international system with anything akin to mutual satisfaction.

Least manifest is the place of less developed countries in alliances designed to facilitate international order or government. Traditionally this has been a function of the alliances of great powers, even when combined with special precautions taken against one great power deemed most likely to generate or diffuse a threat to all. In the nineteenth century, social-revolutionary terror was the prime potential common concern and target for the major powers. Its contemporary equivalents are two. One is nuclear terror, inhering in lesser states or focused in a great power apparently disposed to use nuclear capability as an instrument for gaining ascendancy. Another is intra- or international terrorism resulting from sociopolitical disintegration in less developed areas. The association of lesser states in an alliance structure aimed at dealing with such elementary threats would probably be only indirect. A lesser state typically has only vicarious representation in a great-power concert, mostly by way of some kind of collusion with a friendly or allied great power on issues of particular interest. Having such indirect access to the concert enhances the international status of the lesser country in quite different ways than when it plays off keenly competitive great powers against one another. Moreover, an alliance with a great power may equip a lesser state materially for a key role without disqualifying it politically in the postulated order. The small state may become a mandatory executant of the concert, and consequently an *ad hoc* member of it, in situations of regional disorder which can best be dealt with by a locally congenial power. More generally, the survival of alliances between greater and lesser powers in a concert system introduces particular biases and rigidities to the system, but it also has an advantage. It is apt to minimize the tendency of the lesser states to equate great-power compromises involving small-state interests with deals reached at the expense of lesser states.

Considering the relationship between alliances and different degrees of international order, the findings can be summed up as follows: Alliances between greater and lesser powers are likely to be most useful in implementing an international order that is maintained by interstate restraint, surveillance, intervention, legitimation, and other forms of "control." In systems built around a preponderant power, the result may be an informal imperial order implemented in great measure by means of alliances. Alliances between great and small powers are apt to play the least significant role in relation to a higher level of international order among sovereign states — the level of great-power concert which is dependent upon alignments among great powers for its three main functional prerequisites: diversification of great-power conflicts, diplomatic containment of forward powers, and compensation of thwarted powers. By contrast, the future role of alliances between greater and lesser powers is least predictable when it comes to the question of the material basis of any formalized order. Such material basis consists of the balance of countervailing power and traditionally has been structured by conflicts and administered by mutual-assistance alliances.

Minimum order in the evolving international environment cannot fully depend on either the reciprocally stalemated superpowers or the controlling and ordering role of one of them. As a result, local or regional, and locally or regionally managed, subsystems of minimum order become significant. So do alliances among smaller states, not only because of their value to these states, but also because of the opportunities and limitations such alliances create for great-power involvement.

III.

REGIONAL SUBSYSTEMS AND SUBREGIONAL UNIONS: ALLIANCES OF SMALL POWERS

Alliances among less developed countries cannot matter much as contributions to world order if they are mere extensions of great power policies or if they serve chiefly to project or purge internal stresses. A positive role will depend largely on two things. One is the extent to which the less developed states can evolve into relatively separate subsystems regionally; the other is their ability to evolve relatively specific foreign policies nationally. In other words, these states must show the capacity to enjoy foreign policy autonomy as a group or groups and to accept the disciplines of a foreign policy grounded in external realities as individual actors.

Autonomy is not hegemony; and both differ from the intermediate status of a country or region contended over by two or more outside powers. What are, first, the structural and, second, the weapons-technological preconditions of autonomy? Small-state subsystems would enjoy a maximum of practically attainable autonomy in a multipower global system combining competition with concert. In such a system the great powers would restrain one another to impede other than collective or mandated interventions in regionally or globally upsetting conflicts. The smaller states' autonomy would be curtailed, but it need not be canceled completely if one power were to exercise regional primacy within limits policed by extraregional powers and, even more patently, if a region were to comprise several greater powers engaged in a contest over primacy. By contrast, a polarized East-West conflict between two or three major powers would be compatible with regional autonomy only provisionally, only until the conflict spread into the particular area, converting it into a hegemonic or intermediate zone. Finally, the established dominance of one world power would make any regional autonomy contingent upon the continued convenience of the global hegemon, although autonomy might be considerable if tolerated as self-equilibrating.

The other class of conditions of autonomy concerns weaponry. Regional autonomy might in principle be maximized by the spread of second-strike nuclear capabilities; such capabilities would tend to discourage extraneous intervention in regional violence on different levels. Conversely, diffusion of primitive, locally and globally destabilizing nuclear capabilities would reduce autonomy and foster external intervention. Finally, reliance on nonnuclear conventional military capabilities by local states would be apt to keep prospects for autonomy (as an alternative to systematic intervention) somewhere between the two extremes. The less developed countries are unlikely to acquire advanced, nondestabilizing nuclear capabilities in the near future; they would stop being less developed countries if they did create them by indigenous means. Consequently, their best practical prospect for autonomy would seem to lie in developing conventional military resources while nuclear weapons are acquired in an orderly manner by major industrial powers.

Autonomy toward the outside requires as a complement a decent measure of self-discipline in foreign policy. This means the capacity to contain shifting and conflicting domestic stresses in the interest of a continuity that reflects the relatively fixed factors of political geography. The less developed countries have displayed an initial penchant for what might be called quasi-parliamentary foreign policy. Such a policy introduces the political style of fluid factions into relations of territorially based states. For results it depends on shiftiness rather than weight, agitation rather than aggression. Quasi-parliamentary foreign policy may hopefully appear in retrospect as a major and innovating achievement by otherwise less developed countries. This would be the case if these countries realized in a preindustrial context the model of international relations (often identified with mature industrial societies) without war and with ample organization. Conversely, however, all the parleying might appear in retrospect as but a preliminary exercise occupying the time before the less developed countries subsided into more conventional international politics. Such politics, ultimately hinging on overt conflict, have in the past been the necessary precondition of enduring nation-building; it would be rash to assume that this is no longer so.

Propagandistic conference has already begun to yield to "secret" diplomacy in relations between less developed countries, thus far largely as a vehicle for attempts to attenuate conflicts. Habitual political styles of the first wave of postindependence elites, inadequacy of warlike resources, and external vetoes on the use of force may not ultimately suffice to stem a drift toward other expressions of statecraft. Some of the traditional motives of conflict and war are doubtless inapplicable to the less developed countries. This is especially true for incentives deriving from warrior-centered, feudal social structures and from dynastic problems of succession to extinct family lines, appanages for junior branches, and the nationalistic overcompensation of dynasties for their foreign origins. But even these historical "causes" may survive in changed external forms. Basic causes of conflicts inherent in the character of the state as a territorial unit with "natural" boundaries and as a power organism (or complex of power entities) with an innate drive to expand so as to survive may assert themselves with growing political consciousness or the need for such consciousness. These causes may be intensified by such issues as succession to semimythical autochthonous empires like that of Ghana, nationalization of foreign ideologies, such as Arab socialism, or the need to employ and distract the contemporary equivalents of unruly knights in shining armor.

Relatively uninhibited foreign relations encompassing conflicts and alliances may be the primary necessity in political development. They supply requisite tension by way of hostility as well as needed relief by way of support, sanctuary for growth, and an elevator for lifting the body politic or the leadership above indigenous resources. In the existing international system the less developed countries have tended to seek support, sanctuary, and elevation in relatively safe ways. They have sought to avoid the risks and liabilities that are implicit in conflicts whose stakes are commensurate with the means available to contestants and whose outcomes are potentially conclusive. The prevailing, though in places receding, tendency has been toward two kinds of hostility. At one extreme was diffuse hostility in regard to colonialism en bloc or as it was incarnated in an *ad hoc* target; at the other extreme was specific hostility among individual anticolonial leaders and supporting cliques. Both kinds of hostility have been losing strength. Anticolonialism (even as redefined into anti-neocolonialism) has been losing plausibility because effective decolonization (in terms of anything like political stability) proved to require the cooperation of the ex-colonial powers, while propagandistic charges of neocolonialism have been progressively extended to encompass manifestly indispensable international mechanisms for economic assistance. The personalized, factional competition among postcolonial leaders of the first wave has been slowly but surely on the way out along with the leaders themselves. Ever more military reformers rose to political authority, in large part in reaction to the wastefulness and unreality of earlier policies. This has tended to bring an initial period of retrenchment in the scope of foreign policy activity and ambition. But, sooner or later, these new leaders will have to relate themselves to the world most immediately around them. They are not likely to provoke military conflicts deliberately as a means of compensating for their failings in civilian government. The nature of their appeal to the country and the degree of efficiency of the military instruments at their disposal militate against such resorts. But they may well find in military alliance a more congenial basis for political, economic, and even quasi-constitutional liaison with kindred regimes than is provided by the interstate organizations designed by leaders bred in metropolitan parliaments and labor organizations. If they do, they are likely to seek to give these alliances some implementation, unlike most of their predecessors.[1]

A network of small-state alliances maintaining an elastic connection with the ex-metropoles or other greater powers would not be without merit. It might supplement the United Nations as a link between the less developed countries and the great-power system. The alliances might bring latent conflicts among lesser states into the open, but they would not actually generate them; they might serve to contain and adjust these conflicts rather than treat them as nonexistent or illegitimate. They would thus lay the bases of an embryonic order for the less developed segment of the international system. If they proved workable, small-state alliances would be preferable to grand designs of regional or continental unity. And they would be an improvement over incessant jockeying for position (within unity schemes and outside them) employing mostly covert and politically uncreative methods of coercion. Parallel or countervailing alliance groups might cut across "logical" areas for economic organizations of the common-market type. But few vast areas are really ready for such organizations in the undeveloped segment; and even in the economically ready Western Europe a military-political underpinning of economic organization has proved indispensable and determining.

The general conditions and ideal expectations sur-

[1] Such predispositions do not rule out the willingness of military or ex-military leaders to go along with "platonic" associations for tactical reasons if these are the only ones to be had locally for the time being. The possibility holds true if one is to judge by the attitude of the ex-military regime in South Korea toward the progressive emasculation of its plan for a regional bloc, which resulted in the largely consultative Asian and Pacific Council in June, 1966.

rounding the alliances of lesser states have been considered. We now turn to an examination of the specific functions, motives, and determinants, as well as the dynamics of such alliances in the more or less remote past.

Traditionally, small-state alliances have not been prominent, nor have they been signally successful in dealing with the internal instability or external insecurity of lesser states. Once threatened, lesser countries tended to gravitate toward even remote great powers rather than toward one another when seeking protection against merely local imperialisms of what were but secondary powers globally, such as Venice in the fifteenth-century Italian system, Denmark or Sweden in the seventeenth-century Northern system, or Italy backing Hungary in interwar Central-Eastern Europe. Occasional leagues of small states were not markedly efficient when seeking to promote "armed" neutrality either on the seas (for example, in the late eighteenth century, counting Russia as a minor naval power) or in continental politics (for example, the interwar Little Entente, to the extent that it had initially experimented with neutrality in regard to great-power contests).

The main reason has to do with the aggregation of power—the basic ground for alliance of any kind of state. The reason is far from invalidated in the case of the less developed countries. Where only lesser states are involved, the aggregation is more likely to be one of weaknesses, compounded by the noncomplementary nature of assets and the divergent nature of interests and apprehensions under stress. Consequently, small-state alliances will fare best against dangers of a special kind. One such danger comes from a local small state whose goals are larger than its means. In such a case the threat tends to dissolve by and of itself and the tendency is merely activated by the show of coordinated opposition (which may save face for the expansionist). Some aspects of this special case may have been operative in Indonesia's confrontation with Malaysia. Another manageable danger is one that is remote or hypothetical. Thus, the states making up the so-called Monrovia group have inclined to band together in the United Nations as a safeguard against demographically based Asian expansion into Africa —a self-defensive move that has been paralleled more recently by the Asian component of the Afro-Asian bloc.[2] Small-state alliances may prove most tempting if they are for offense, however. Offensive alliances are typically directed at a weak spot in the adversary's front. And they are initially capable of aggregating resources and reconciling aims by concentrating on anticipated gains rather than on their distribution in case of success or their reduction in case of failure. The Arab states were able to forget their differences long enough to improvise an alliance against Israel on several occasions. And, to fill the time between the legendary precedent of a joint offensive against colonialism and the mythical prospect of offensive action against South African racism, Black African states may come to implement military (as distinct from planned or political) offensive alliances against one another. Such alignments might even encompass both Asian and African countries and conflicts: the founders of the Casablanca Group sought to effect such linkage on the political level

---

[2] See Doudou Thiam, *The Foreign Policy of African States* (New York: 1965), pp. 58–59, and *The New York Times*, June 17, 1966, p. 8.

and possibly on the paramilitary level when inviting Indonesia to join the organization. Offensive alliances would be justified as holy wars against local accomplices of imperialism. But they would be more authentically inspired by the difficulty of overcoming the prevalent prejudice against changes in the postcolonial territorial status quo.

Less developed small countries might also find applications of the second major ground for alliance—control, including restraint. An alliance for control, however, is likely to be only an improvised and relatively platonic one. One might cite here the restraint exerted by Iran on Pakistan as a fellow-Muslim and sympathetically disposed power during the fighting with India. It will not be frequent, however, that any but a great power would rate its stake in the existing order so highly as to incur the liabilities of alliance for the sole or main purpose of gaining access to restraint or surveillance over another state. The Philippines, Malaysia, and Thailand may have shared the desire of the new Indonesian leaders to hem in and otherwise enfold post-Sukarno Indonesia internationally. Such restraint may thus have been one incentive behind plans for expanding the Association of Southeast Asia, while another would be the desire to create a respectable basis for externally aided development and the rudiments of possible future defense against China or any other domineering regional power. So far, reciprocal restraints have been most prominent in associations of less developed countries aimed at mutual assurance against subversion effected by harboring political exiles of and against one another. Commitments designed to deal with this most keenly felt threat to many an African regime have smacked of the

Italian Renaissance even more than of the cold war.[3] The undertaking seemed worthwhile, even if it did not ensure actual assistance against subversion. (It would seem that the Ivory Coast government failed to aid the allied civilian regime in Upper Volta against the military overthrow in early 1966.)

The last category of alliance motives concerns international order or government. Alliances and alignments underlying sundry regional or continental associations, unions, or concerts—such as the Organization of African Unity, most prominently, and, even more recently, the Asian and Pacific Council—belong in this group. So far, this kind of association has flourished most in Africa. Its pursuit helped to dilute hegemonic contests over potentially forcible unification into contests over leadership in a superficially voluntary unity. The multipurpose associations have stressed political, economic, cultural, and other cooperation but have not been strong on security. In what might be called cryptoalliances, a plethora of conspicuous politico-economic activities and organizational features overlay a not too solid military component (for example, the Casablanca Group, the Southeast Asia Association). And there have been pseudointegrated alliances, featuring joint general staffs and commands but little individual or collective military capability (for example, the African Malagasy Union, the Conseil de l'Entente).

For the time being, it might appear advantageous for less developed countries either to play down the

---

[3] The issue may be temporarily of decreasing gravity. See I. William Zartman, "Characteristics of Developing Foreign Policies," in William H. Lewis, ed., *French-Speaking Africa* (New York: 1965), p. 190.

military alliance aspect or to express it chiefly in institutions paralleling those for political and economic cooperation. These countries may thus go through the motions of some not too provocative alliance- or alignment-making in a world which is either ostensibly foeless (military conflict being unlikely, disapproved of, or both, as in Black Africa) or manifestly too dangerous (the chief threat or target being unmanageable by regional resources activated thus far, as in South Asia and South Africa). Moreover, while busy associating among themselves, the less developed countries may continue to derive their real security, both internal and external, from markedly unintegrated and even merely *de facto* alliances with extraregional great powers, the United States in Asia and the French or British ex-metropoles in Africa. It may be significant that Upper Volta, which appeared to depend on African allies for security, differed from these allies by not having a bilateral alliance with France. Even when the defense pact with the ex-metropole had been abrogated, as in the case of Nigeria, the agreement could be said to have continued substantially in effect. Thus, a small-state association in South Asia may likewise facilitate the transfer of chief responsibility for military security to an ex-metropole in due course—for example, to Japan in regard to South Korea by giving Seoul a more secure basis from which to activate relations with Tokyo.[4]

What, then, about the dynamics of regional groupings and alliances of lesser states? In Africa there has

---

[4] See Hanspeter F. Strauch, *Panafrika* (Zurich: 1964), pp. 115–16; Arnold Rivkin, *The African Presence in World Affairs* (New York: 1963), p. 170; and James W. Morley, *Japan and Korea* (New York: 1965), pp. 56–66, respectively.

been more reciprocal stimulation than consolidation. The chief political function of these impermanent and unstable alignments seems to have been to animate adverse formations before dissolving to make way for ever new and, so far, more inclusive unions. The reason lay in the largely personal, accidental, and opportunistic nature of the motives responsible for particular alignments. These could override the more general or objective alliance determinants in a situation displaying few military threats to national security, a limited capacity to pool either internal resources or external ambitions, and a great diversity of both ambitions and threats to regime security. Even where a territorial conflict did appear to break out, for example, between two members of the defense arrangements of the African and Malagasy Union, it was apparently simulated as a cover for the real conflict over a change in government in Dahomey, which was unwelcome to the leader of Niger.[5] The relatively acute character of the territorial, ethnic, and religious conflict dividing Somalia from Ethiopia (and, in some of these respects, Kenya) has been so far an exception in Africa, just as the explosion of the Pakistani-Indian conflict has been exceptional in Asia. Likewise unusual has been the conjunction of economic and security incentives tying together the Conseil de l'Entente around a relatively strong economic power's, the Ivory Coast's, underwriting a "solidarity fund"; an apparently serious adversary, the now defunct Union of African States (Ghana, Guinea, Mali); and the tangible and manageable task of protecting a landlocked enclave, Upper Volta, from either absorption by the adversary grouping or defection to it. The Association of

[5] Strauch, *op. cit.,* p. 121.

Southeast Asia, comprising the Philippines, Thailand, and Malaysia, initially facing Indonesia and in the future perhaps encompassing her, is the nearest example of such a relatively small and tight multipurpose association of lesser powers in Asia. It has been backed by the United States in somewhat the same comparatively discreet manner as the African counterpart has been backed by France.

By and large, small-state groupings in the less developed segment have tended or tried to be ostensibly for something—say, economic and political cooperation or unity—and against no one. They thus attempt to reverse the traditionally more familiar thrust of alliances against someone or something and only incidentally for anything positive. Consequently, the impact of concrete crises has tended to scramble alignments (in Africa) or deactivate them (in Asia). It remains to be seen whether determinants will grow less accidental and alliances more stable as regional conditions crystallize. This might result from the emergence of an avowable enemy in Africa, such as white racism, and of a both manifest and manageable threat in South Asia, such as Vietnamese, as distinct from Chinese, local imperialism. Or there might evolve a network of intercountry conflicts variously related to the above factors. Such conflicts would tend to substitute traditionally more commonplace outflanking alignments for subregional associations of geographically contiguous states, which have been propounded in Africa as the only legitimate ones and favored in South Asia by geographic and political accidents. Greater stability and more predictability of alignments and orientations in the undeveloped segment thus may well be inseparable from the short-range liability of specific conflicts, more intense than before though still not very large-scale.

In any event, the less developed countries of today and tomorrow are unlikely to transcend the limitations inherent in small-state alliances as a category. Such alliances, therefore, could not soon become self-sufficient bases of regional orders or primary instruments of great-power politics. They might, however, usefully supplement other instrumentalities of security and order endowed with larger scope (the United Nations) or more concentrated power (the major states and their alliances). The issue bears on a basic ambivalence in the relationship between small states and the great powers. Small-state alliances are at once a means for keeping the great powers and their conflicts "out" of a region and a means for attenuating or concealing the fact of the great powers' being "in" as the ultimately indispensable or unextrudable makeweights and safeguards. The African experience has not been unique in this respect. Moreover, this ambivalence of the lesser powers has a counterpart for the great powers in the uncertain balance between opportunities and liabilities implicit in small-state alliances.

On the positive side, opportunities have to do mainly with the problem of access. Small-state alliances can supply major powers with a facility for both access to a region and limited disengagement from it. Access is facilitated whenever an informal relationship between a major power and a "multilateral" small-state association is less neocolonial on the face of it than an unequal bilateral alliance would be. Having a special connection with any of the members of a small-state alliance, moreover, may help the greater power in diffusing influence toward the otherwise less accessible members. Military access supplements political access whenever the major power can use, in an emergency, the infrastructures that were built ostensibly by and for the multination alliance. To the extent that having a part in generating local strength can be expected to preserve access to ways and means of influencing or backing its employment, the interested great power can safely reduce its conspicuous presence. A partial disengagement in a period of relative quiet will in any event be useful and may even be necessary to make something closely resembling an effective alliance of smaller states feasible and imperative in local terms.

On the negative side are the liabilities connected with the degree and timing of great-power involvement. The great power indirectly associated with a small-state alliance risks being drawn into a new category of conflicts and problems involving the member-countries in the process of keeping the alliance going. By contrast, it risks being kept out of intrinsically more serious issues to the extent that the small-state allies develop collective strength and a spirit of autonomy. Overinvolvement in issues affecting alliance cohesion, but not affecting American security in any but the most indirect way, is apt to be taxing for the United States in the less developed areas. But it is unlikely to be any more taxing than apparently premature or excessive exclusion—if American reactions to de Gaulle's policy in Europe supply any guidance. A related danger is that of an overly delayed re-engagement, possibly past the point of the virtual collapse of the small-state alliance. The alliance would be to blame insofar as its existence had discouraged the more or less self-effacing, or excluded, sponsor from an early resort to deterrent demonstrations or defense actions. This might happen out of consideration for the local legitimacy of the small-state alliance. Or the alliance might merely supply a convenient pretext for inaction, just as its creation may have been no more than a substitute for vigorous or sustained military action at an earlier stage.

It seems safe to draw only a trite conclusion about this last issue in any presently conceivable world order. Small-state attitudes and great-power dilemmas being what they are, differences between alliances which do and those which do not formally include great powers alongside the lesser ones will continue to be at once tenuous and significant. The resulting choices for the United States will be correspondingly precarious but also important.[6]

---

[6] An explicit discussion of American policies for the less developed world is presented in the author's *Imperial America,* especially on pp. 83ff.

IV. CONCLUSION

In one form or another, alliances are here to stay—and those between great powers and small and developing powers more certainly than any others. Compared with the long history and likely future of alliances, contrary devices like neutralism appear only fleetingly in history as tactical adjustments to transient international configurations of power and as insufficient remedies for deep-lying internal deficiencies and dislocations.

But, like all traditional institutions in changing conditions, alliances must undergo subtle changes in both conception and implementation. The constitutions of states have tended to evolve from unwritten to written ones as new actors and forces pressed into the traditional political process and had to be circumscribed by law pending their being controlled or canceled by conditions. Conversely, as ever-new actors and forces thrust themselves or are projected into international politics, the evolution of alliances —another institutional embodiment of checks and balances—may be from written and explicit instruments to unwritten and only implicitly contracted stipulations. The essential point is not the form but the fact of a continued, and perhaps increasing, need for constraints on disorder to supplement weak legal restraints and to shield somewhat the realistic degree of independence of small and new states from oppression by greater power and decomposition into still smaller and chaotic fragments of power.

Just as written and even unwritten constitutions

are only as effective as the conventional practice they would stabilize and the structure of social power and political interests that undergirds them, so are alliances dependent on such extraneous factors. Their everyday role is limited, like that of constitutions, and should be unobtrusive; the need for explicitly affirming or invoking either a constitution or an alliance is a certain sign of some kind of crisis. As institutional stabilizers of political behavior, however, fostering the growth of conventions and reducing the impact of outright coercion, alliances fulfill as vital a role in international relations as any other institutional instrument so far developed for controlling man's acts and environment in other spheres of politics. To take such a view of alliances liberates one from automatically equating constitutional order within states with juridically closed systems of international organization among states. The way to close the alleged gap between technological innovation and institutional stagnation in international life is not necessarily to invent new and more authoritative institutions; it is rather to manage old ones with growing sophistication. International politics of and for a world order in which part of the burden of responsibility rests on alliances is an art to be learned in time as a matter of a nation's foreign-policy tradition as much as it is initially an emergency course decided upon as a matter of one or another statesman's judgment and will.